T0194505

CONGRATULATIONS GRADUATE!
YOU HAVE ARRIVED AT THE BEACH

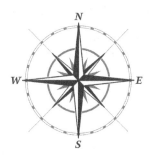

NAVIGATING FROM THE BEACH
TO THE BOARDROOM

TAMERA FOLEY, PhD
SHARON WADDLE, PhD

WESTBOW
PRESS®
A DIVISION OF THOMAS NELSON
& ZONDERVAN

WestBow Press books may be ordered through booksellers or by contacting:

WestBow Press
A Division of Thomas Nelson & Zondervan
1663 Liberty Drive
Bloomington, IN 47403
www.westbowpress.com
1 (866) 928-1240

Scriptures taken from the Holy Bible, New International Version®, NIV®. Copyright © 1973, 1978, 1984, 2011 by Biblica, Inc.™ Used by permission of Zondervan. All rights reserved worldwide. www.zondervan.com The "NIV" and "New International Version" are trademarks registered in the United States Patent and Trademark Office by Biblica, Inc.™

ISBN: 978-1-9736-7512-9 (sc)
ISBN: 978-1-9736-7511-2 (e)

Library of Congress Control Number: 2019915551

Print information available on the last page.

WestBow Press rev. date: 10/02/2019

Navigating Beach Life

Today I graduate and move to the beach.
I'm so excited about what life will be.
I swim to the edge and dream of bright and blue things.
I'm so thrilled about it all, I simply dance and sing.

I glance at the fish and glean in the sand. I watch
for the whales and put my sunglasses on. The sky is
so rich, the ocean blue; Starfish in all colors and
seashells on shore, I wonder just when my ship will soar.

For a moment I ponder what's in store
for me or does my shipwreck end
as in 400 BC and nothing happens at the
bottom of the Black Sea.

My plans are clear – My future is bright.
I run to the hut to get more delight.
I lounge on the beach chair and sip on the
brew, I'm living the life everyone wants to do.

I dry off and shiver at the end of the day,
praying that God will make a way
for this beach life getaway to simply transcend,
because I want this beach life to never end.

Congrats Graduate. You are living the Beach Life!

—Dr. Sharon Waddle

Special Graduation Message

from parents, family, teachers, administrators, neighbors,
mentors, employers, co-workers and friends

Graduate Name: _____

_____

_____

_____

_____

_____

_____

_____

_____

_____

_____

Signature/Title: _____

Date: _____

Navigating from the Beach to the Boardroom

Congratulations and Best Wishes in Life!

Tamera L. Foley

Sharon D. Waddle

Tamera L. Foley, PhD   Sharon D. Waddle, PhD

Educational Consultant   Industrial Organizational Psychologist

DEDICATION

We dedicate this book to all graduating high school seniors, college graduates, graduates completing terminal degrees and all scholars who desire to learn basic principles to live a life of continual success.

We dedicate this book to all Church Organizations, all School Systems and all Healthcare Organizations and Corporations who will nurture and train new graduates to become aligned with their purpose and positions in life.

We dedicate this book to every student who has a yearning to become leaders and propel this nation to a level of integrity and empowerment to surpass the limitations of our past and move forward to a blessed and dynamic future.

We dedicate this book to those who have lost their pathway in life and want to be restored and catapult into an explosive and amazing future.

We dedicate this book to all aspiring spiritual leaders and world leaders, who want to bring ultimate sovereignty to the nations and creations of God almighty.

We dedicate this book to everyone who makes it possible to go from the beach to the boardroom.

PREFACE

Congratulations Graduate! You Have Arrived at the Beach was written as a strategic plan for students who are graduating every day and may need encouragement and guidance as they journey to the next phase of their life. As a psychologist and educator, we have seen students over the years that need more information to assist them.

It is our desire that the students will share this information with their families, friends, and loved ones. We wanted to ensure that the information was relevant and addressed life in a holistic manner. This book card is unique as its information can be used now and in the future. The book card is not one to place in a drawer but can be kept handy and utilized as a quick reference for practical awareness that leads you to journey from the Beach to the Boardroom.

We chose the Beach as it has a calming effect on people. It is where people go to retreat. It is a place of joy, laughter, fun, excitement, and relaxation. It takes a great deal of planning and transition to get to the Beach. Everyone can go to the beach, but not everyone understands the possibilities of how to get to the final destination of beach type living. The Beach is a platform for rejuvenation to excel in life.

We are honored to share this new and innovative greeting card booklet that can remain a keepsake for a lifetime.

TABLE OF CONTENTS

CONGRATULATIONS GRADUATE

What an exciting day! You have accomplished so much over the years. You are now moving to your next life's adventure. How does that feel? Are you numb without feelings? Are you feeling energized? Are you excited to leave school? Are you happy that there will be a big celebration in your honor? Today may also be a bit overwhelming. You may wonder, "Have I made any choices that affect my future? Did I make the right choice?". Whatever the answer, you have time to make different choices. Be bold in your decisions. Whether you choose to further your education through college, technical school, career, or being an entrepreneur, you can achieve greatness. Your attitude determines your altitude. How high you fly in the parachute of life depends on you.

Steve Jobs spoke at the Stanford University Commencement ceremony in 2014. His most notable statement was (Garnett, 2019), "I'm convinced that the only thing that kept me going was that I loved what I did. You've got to find what you love. And that is as true for your work as it is for your lovers. Your work is going to fill a large part of your life, and the only way to be truly satisfied is to do what you believe is great work. And the only way to do great work is to love what you do. If you haven't found it yet, keep looking. Don't settle."

Toni Morrison was the commencement speaker at Wellesley College in 2014. Her most notable statement (Garnett, 2019) was, "Being your own story means you can always choose the tone. It also means that you can invent the language to say who you are and what you mean ... I see your life as already artful, waiting, just waiting and ready for you to make it art."

These tips may help you remain focused on your journey. How will you serve the world? What is it in you that the world needs? You have something that the world needs. Grab it and never let it go!

Prayers and blessings on your graduation and in your future life.

A GRADUATES' PRAYER

Thank you, God, for this opportunity to show my gratitude for your direction and support during my years of education and learning to be a student among scholars. Thank you for allowing me to complete the assignments that were required to achieve approval to move forward towards commencement. I am grateful that you made me a priority and you gave me the ability to retain information that I was taught. Lord I am grateful for the many hidden treasures that you revealed on my journey towards graduation. I looked for favor and you provided; I looked for peace and you offered it freely; I desired joy and you held me up under many adverse circumstances and I'm thankful. I needed understanding and you gave me knowledge and equipped me to share with others. I am grateful for the support of family, friends, teachers, role models and school administrators.

As I enter into a world of mysteries, I ask you to give me the plan that you desire for my life; Compel me to operate in integrity with all mankind; Help me to fulfill my assignments and my purpose. God, I desire to be steadfast and focused on the journey that you have for me. Give me the skills to become a world leader with sovereignty, power and greatness. I ask to always abide in your presence and dwell in your love. Renew me and restore me each day that I may cover the territory that you designed for me to rule and reign. In Jesus Name. Amen

CONGRATULATIONS GRADUATE!

YOU HAVE ARRIVED AT THE BEACH

NAVIGATING FROM THE BEACH
TO THE BOARDROOM

Part I: Creating Your
Integrity Brand

TAMERA FOLEY, PhD • SHARON WADDLE, PhD

PART I

Creating Your Integrity Brand

Each of us are uniquely different and represent a standard of being that is exclusive and compelling. You have a lot to offer the world and the world will embrace the goods and services that you bring that represent what you are about. Too often we compare ourselves to others and want to be more popular, more attractive, more charismatic and more gifted. The most important thing is to simply be you because no one has what you have, and no one can do some of the things that you can achieve or bring to the table of life. Respecting who you are, owning who you are and empowering yourself is the greatest gift that you can give to yourself.

In order to create your brand, you must first own it as Daymond Johns (Shark Tank) owned the company FUBU. He had a determination to go beyond the walls of who he was to create a dynasty that also reaches back and pulls up others. Branding is important because it shows value and it shows ownership. Farmers brand their cattle so that if they wander to new territory, there will be no mistake that the cow belongs to his farm business. Without branding, you could develop and incur cost of living to raise up a herd of cattle and another person can take possession, own and sell what you nurtured and cared for.

As a brand of integrity, you should honor yourself, have dignity, honesty and never take advantage of others. As a person with integrity you must be careful not to allow others to sell you out because you are not property and should never be sold. Once you know, create and take a stand for who you are, there is an invisible brand surrounding your disposition that tells people that you are comfortable with yourself and you are strong in the essence of who you are created to be. There is an unspoken countenance that says, "I accept myself and I have no qualms about who I am and there is no comparison to who you are".

Branding includes self-awareness, self-knowledge, ownership, fortitude, dignity, purpose, power, planning, perseverance and overflowing. A strong brand is well nourished, nurtured and becomes imminent and a perpetual trend setter. Some brands are bold and compelling, and some brands are quiet and focused, yet still effective human beings.

You were created as a brilliant idea, so it's important to know that you exist to manifest the greatness that you were designed to project.

1. Look in the mirror and know who you are internally and externally.
2. Accept who you are and learn to thrive in it.
3. Stick with the plan of who God made you to be.
4. Continually empower yourself to learn and stand firm in your beliefs.
5. Ensure that your power is directed towards an arena whereby you can support a legacy that extends who you are born to be.
6. Make daily plans to walk in your brand of humanity and pursue until you overflow, and the goodness is birth in others that surrounds you.

Congratulations, your brand looks good on you!

CONGRATULATIONS GRADUATE!

YOU HAVE ARRIVED AT THE BEACH

NAVIGATING FROM THE BEACH
TO THE BOARDROOM

Part II: Socialization and Communication Etiquettes

TAMERA FOLEY, PhD • SHARON WADDLE, PhD

PART II

Socialization and Communication Etiquettes

How important is your social life? A social life is the part of a person's time spent doing enjoyable things with others. A social life can assist in improving your mental health, as noted in "Building Better Mental Health", Axner, (1993). Social connections are important throughout life. It is important to make healthy social connections to enhance your social life.

As you journey into the next phase of your life, you may or may not keep the same social network. You may lose some old friends and find some new ones. In any case, make a decision to keep them positive. It is wonderful to laugh and have fun throughout your life.

A Social Life Is Significant as described by Melanie Gray (2015) at Hampton University because "It provides a balance, helps you form good relationships, expands your identity and broadens your horizon". If you have already had the opportunities to travel outside of your community and/or country, you have begun to broaden your horizons. Seeing how other cultures live and do things are just a few ways to broaden your horizons.

Every person you come in contact with serves a purpose in your life. Some of them will be in your life for a short time while others will be there for a lifetime. Embrace the positive relationships and learn from them. In your future life, how can your brand open the door for opportunities?

Being socially aware may give you favor above others. Being a good listener, paying close attention to what other have to say, thinking about how others may react to what you say and do are important factors of social awareness. Improving in this area opens the door for your connection to humanity and empowers you to be sought after in the social arena of life.

Social Media

Social media allows people to interact and share contacts as well as interests. Social media can also help strengthen family ties and connections. It is imperative to maintain a balance in this area. Do you spend more time on social media than with those you love?

Although social media is a major part of life human interaction is also important throughout life. Choose wisely your social interactions and how you utilize social media. The choices you make will have a lasting effect on your life. Ensure that you are in control of your social activity, social life, and social media.

Friendship and Dating

Good friendships require spending quality time and making an exchange, showing care and interest in the life and concerns of the other person and being transparent and sharing your life interest with them. Many friends will remain for a lifetime and others will fade away. Enjoy people and family connections but allow them to evolve so that you connect with people who are a good fit for you. High school friends may remain dormant, but some will come back later in life (some sooner). College friends likewise may end with college, but there are special friends who will remain close to your heart even when you have not spoken in years. These friends may show up in your life 20 years later and you will be able to resume the friendship as though it never stopped.

Dating pulls more on the emotional strings of the heart particularly at the beginning and at the ending of an intimate friendship. Be prepared to live,

7

laugh, and love, but when it is time to move on, plan to be mature and courteous. The sooner you can close the door to an unhealthy relationship, will allow a new door to open. This time, you will be wiser and smarter and know exactly what to look for. I often tell my brother to weed out quickly when you get warning signs that are not conducive to your health and well-being. Learn from past mistakes and be the best friend that you can be.

Verbal Communication

Communicating effectively is important for all graduates and all people. Verbalizing clearly and concisely with patience and respect is very important to sustain good social relationships.

Telephone Etiquette

Practicing proper telephone etiquette when utilizing the cell phone (text messages), emails and other mobile devices are also very important. It is easy to be more aloof over the phone, but we must maintain an orderly conversation to avoid offensive behaviors.

Email Communication

Emails are mostly used for communication in business but may also be used to share information with friends and family. When you receive an email, please think carefully about whether you need to reply or prefer to speak to the person very diplomatically face to face. Never feel pressured to respond back. Some conversations are more appropriate in person.

It is imperative to keep in mind that the tone of the email is determined by the receiver of the email. It is important that you take the time to read the email aloud so you can hear any tone that you may or may not intend to send. This will also assist in hearing the language, so it is not sarcastic or demeaning in any way to the receiver.

Gaming

Many people enjoy gaming as a hobby, sport, and professionally. However, remember to be polite. You may be playing with children, so it is important to practice good language (meaning no swearing on inappropriate words).

As with all sports, congratulate your opponent at the end of the game and do not stop the game because you are angry. Practice good sportsmanship.

Mute your microphone if you are playing music or if there is distracting background noise. Also, do not cheat, be respectful and be a good sport.

Remember these are skills that take you from the beach to the boardroom. Enjoy the journey!

CONGRATULATIONS GRADUATE!

YOU HAVE ARRIVED AT THE BEACH

NAVIGATING FROM THE BEACH
TO THE BOARDROOM

Part III: Choosing A
Career that Feels Like
Another Day at the Beach

TAMERA FOLEY, PhD • SHARON WADDLE, PhD

PART III

Choosing A Career that Feels Like Another Day at the Beach

After graduation there are so many choices to make. The idea of working a few years after graduation, may be an option to consider. Enrolling in a community college or trade school may be considered, going to a university or specialty school may be your focus or you may decide that you are ready to be a soldier and visit the headquarters for the Airforce, Navy, Army or Marines. Some choose to multi-task by working and taking a couple classes. Talk with your family or mentor about it because the sky is the limit of the possibilities available to you.

Some graduates set goals that they will go straight to a 4-year college institution and remain enrolled until they complete a doctoral degree. Others may want to work a couple years and take a couple classes here and there. Some people want to enroll in specialty schools to be a designer, a chef or perhaps a real estate agent. Enrolling in an apprenticeship program as a journeyman, draftsman or welding et al may be desirable. The choice is yours and you can be equally successful in any career that you select.

What were you born to do? What is your greatest desire? Where do you want to travel in life? What beaches do you want to experience?

Immediately Going into the Workforce

The workforce is a beach that gives immediate monetary gratification. It provides independence earlier but may or may not start with a lower pay grade. If you are blessed to find a high paying job this may be where you decide to remain. If you go to the workforce without a college degree, you may discover later that there are management jobs that you will never qualify for without a college degree. Maybe that's okay with you because not everyone wants to be in management or work at a desk.

College Bound Journey

If your choice is to leave home immediately and go to a college out of state or in state, you will find that you have to grow up quickly and step up to the plate of meeting all of your daily needs. If you are easily distracted and parents are in agreement, perhaps you may need to stay home and commute to college the first year or two until you become more grounded. Talking to an enrollment counselor and taking career assessment tests at the local college or university may help you make this important life career choice.

Apprenticeship Programs

Specialty schools will allow you to gain certified skills quickly that enables you to go to work in your designated field within a couple of years. Some apprenticeship programs can be completed in six months and can vary from six weeks to two years typically.

Military Choices

Many enroll in the military because they have a legacy from family members or friends who were successful, and the passion has crossed over into their minds. It's important to visit all of the headquarters and learn about each branch of the military to determine which is best for you and what benefits are important to you. If you are the adventurous one this choice will open up a world of travel opportunities immediately.

Self-Employment/Family Business

Some have businesses already started that they want to pursue and enhance. If your passion lies within your personal business and you have a good business plan and a vision for future success, we congratulate you on taking this path and encourage you to periodically attend conferences and work sessions so that you remain abreast of the changing demands in your field.

Music and Arts Industry

Many of you have multiple creative gifts and are ready to become artist in the music, dance or entertainment industry. If you are ready to soar and there is no stopping you, then find at least two mentors who are in agreement with you to move forward towards your goals and dreams. If your talent needs refinement, consider enrolling in the fine arts schools to develop your purpose and skills. Making decisions like these can be stressful and exciting at the same time, but it's your life and you get to choose because you are now preparing for the type of life that you want to live.

Choosing a career is a bold move. You are excited yet a little apprehensive. Your choices may change over the years. How do you know what you would like to do?

Career Assessments

Many career quizzes are available online to test your career preferences based on your skills and interests. Colleges and universities will assist you with taking a career assessment appropriate to your needs. Options may include: *The Kuder Career Assessment; Motivational Appraisal Potential Performance (MAPP); Myers-Briggs Strong Interest Inventory; MyNextMove and the Predictive Index Behavioral Assessment. It is important to:*

1. "Know your strengths, values, personality, and skills" (2018). It will help you learn about yourself.
2. Learn about all of your options and which one you think may satisfy you.
3. "Make a Good Decision" - Learn all you can about the choices that interest you.

Here are a few things to consider (Gray, 2015):

1. "Happiness" - Is this a career that you like and will make you happy?
2. "Marketability"- Is there a market now and in the future for this craft?
3. "Social Environment" - Think about a career that fits your social needs.
4. "Work Style"- We all work differently. Choose a career that is conducive to how you like to work.
5. "Priorities"- Make a list of your top priority. Is this career in alignment?

Once you choose a career that you enjoy, every day will feel like you are living a beach day. It will feel satisfying and enjoyable. Have a wonderful beach life!

CONGRATULATIONS GRADUATE!

YOU HAVE ARRIVED AT THE BEACH

NAVIGATING FROM THE BEACH
TO THE BOARDROOM

Part IV: The Beach and the Boardroom

TAMERA FOLEY, PhD • SHARON WADDLE, PhD

PART IV

The Beach and the Boardroom

The beach and the boardroom represent a dichotomy in most languages and yet they have similarities that empowers us for a lifetime of success and achievements. The beach and boardroom in harmony represents a balance of work and play and creating a mindset that they are not mutually exclusive.

The boardroom comes with many perks and benefits that creates value to our lifestyles and helps us to plan effectively for good living and raising children and families. The boardroom propels us to walk in integrity, creativity and leadership roles.

Many entrepreneurs now carry laptops to the beach as a standard work place, in order to enjoy the best of both worlds. A true entrepreneur can master the unsupervised work demands and maintain a rhythm of accomplishments from any environment. Employees who are technically savvy can work from anywhere, anytime because they have the tools to be efficient in any environment that they roam. Hotels and resorts have business centers and equipment to ensure audio visual needs are met. Camping sites are filled with connections for electrical plug ins and airplanes and airports have a wealth of hospitality areas to accommodate any personal or business needs. This brand of working without walls gives more freedom to the workplace and sets the stage for a new level of creativity.

The beach is a place of serenity, light heartedness and gentle effects to have fun and shed the cares of life. The beach can be any location that creates this atmosphere of joy and refreshment. The beach is a place that we daydream about when times are hard, and the load is heavy to carry. The beach is filled with good memories, refreshing beverages, good food, people who are carefree, light and airy sand to play in, lounge chairs, beach umbrellas, beach balls and ocean water that lulls us to sleep and takes us to a place of escape, jubilance and exhilaration. The beach keeps us sane and healthy in our minds because it opens the pressure value and allows us to exhale.

The Boardroom is used to represent the workplace in whatever form, venue or atmosphere that your path takes you. Typically, the boardroom is associated with pressure, heavy and complicated work assignments, getting dirty and getting dumped on. It represents a place filled with challenges and competitive spirits that wreak havoc on persons who consider themselves small in the scheme of things and on the organizational flow chart. Most people want to be anywhere but in the boardroom in the lime light, in the hot chair or in the pigeon's seat. The good news is that as you grow, you will thrive in the boardroom and what once appeared to be a challenge is now just another day at the beach. In this phase of workplace dynamics, you now are strong and courageous, and you are seasoned to withstand pressure and welcome the opportunity to shine. As a seasoned worker, you are fit for the assignment and you are excited to let the boardroom umbrella reach to the highest level of opportunity. You don't mind the sand blowing in your face because as a seasoned employee you are prepared and ready to face the needs of the day.

Your boardroom and your beach may offer the same accommodations but until you arrive make certain to enjoy the best of both worlds to maintain a great and harmonious lifestyle.

Congratulations graduate! You have arrived at the beach.

CONGRATULATIONS GRADUATE!

YOU HAVE ARRIVED AT THE BEACH

NAVIGATING FROM THE BEACH
TO THE BOARDROOM

Part V: Healthy Living
for New Graduates

TAMERA FOLEY, PhD • SHARON WADDLE, PhD

PART V

Healthy Living for New Graduates

As a new graduate, you are facing a new level of independence and may need some practical guidelines to prepare to make good decisions that will propel you to enjoy good health and well-being. Healthy living encompasses physical health, mental health, personal hygiene, medicinal treatments, exercise, dietary intake, responsible libation and chemical substance usage. Healthy living sets a standard for more invitations to graduation parties and social events.

Physical Health is Necessary for Healthy Living

It's important to take care of your physical health and make decisions that will allow you to have healthcare insurance and healthcare benefits for your family network. Often employers provide healthcare benefits as part of the hiring package. This employee healthcare is very valuable and typically has a value that supplements your salary by 10-20 thousand dollars. It's very important to respect this package because it allows you to maintain healthy minds, healthy bodies and dental treatments that keeps a beautiful smile in place. Many people neglect dental health and are taxed with costly remedies later in life. Being proactive with healthcare will allow you to have the best life possible and enjoy fun in the sun. Regular check-ups and follow up care allows us to maintain health and prevent illness and infirmity that slows down your life.

Mental Health is Vital for the Soul to Flourish

Mental healthcare is vital for your spiritual and emotional well-being and allows you to resume a better quality of life. Thereby you can focus in school, on your jobs and in your family living and lifestyle. When mental health suffers, it impacts all of your connections and support systems and it decreases the quality of your life. It's necessary to be bold and courageous to seek the healthcare you need and have no reservations because it is just as important as breathing. Many people give up because they can't find an immediate cure and they may feel worse on the regimens provided. Never the less, take heart and be vigilant to get the care you need because you are just that important to weather the storm. Doctors are practicing and can only prescribe based on what they know. Communicating effectively and frequently is very important to ensure you get the regimen and specific care that will support your needs. Healthy thinking, speaking and decisions will support your mental health. Considering the challenges others are facing will allow you to overlook some of the triggers that are based on mental illness and not a direct insult or attack against you personally. There are challenges everywhere, so be careful to treat people with respect and dignity because their unexpected short fuses and tempers are never about you but, has root in the issues that they are faced with in their lives.

A healthy mind is important to a life of joy and happiness. Having a good sense of humor, a good self-image and rest will support a healthy mindset and allow you to be at peace.

Personal Hygiene Enhances your Support System

It's nice to sit beside a person when they have just cleaned up with a fresh shower, left the hair salon, barber shop, nail spa or sauna. There is a new aroma that penetrates the environment and allows you to know the person has a standard of hygiene that reflects their care for themselves and their sense of self-preservation. A neat and well-groomed appearance brings up your popularity score and invites a network of friends into your circle of life that ensure you have a support system in place. In many cases family members can provide the services needed to assist with proper hygiene care, when you communicate how important it is to you.

Oral hygiene is important and can prevent cold and flu that may lead to other dreaded diseases. Taking care of your teeth allows you to eat all of the foods that you enjoy and enhances your ability to chew and savor special meals and outings. Grooming is essential to daily connections and invitations to events and community activities. The more you care for yourself, the more people will care to include you in their activities in the community. Good personal hygiene enhances your self-respect and elevates your value and inclusion.

Medicinal Treatment Elevates Your Ability to Thrive

Medications are prescribed to treat signs and symptoms of infirmity. When we take medications for specific reasons, we need to document whether the benefits are significant when the treatment has ended. If there was a cough, did the medication resolve the cough? When we have done our part to take the medications on schedule, we should see results. If the problem continues, there may be times that the medication was not effective because other factors hindered the treatment from working properly. Circumstances change and we must communicate to our healthcare providers any variable that we did not provide to assist them with making the best treatment choices on your behalf. Sometimes the process is repetitive, but your healthcare is important enough to pursue continual adjustments as needed. Healthy living requires us to flex our muscles and try every avenue to achieve success.

Exercise and Fitness Re-energize You for the Challenges in Life

Exercising may not give the ambiance that we enjoy, but it certainly builds strength and character. It's important to persevere with the task at hand but at the end of the session, a good shower and hygiene care will maintain your friends and supports. Exercising not only helps the body, but it also restores the mind. Exercise gives us energy and more stamina to deal with life. It allows us to sleep better and be available for issues in life that develop unexpectedly. Meditation and exercise keeps the heart young and allows us to soar in life.

Dietary Intake Provides Strength and Vitality

Food is medicine for the soul and health and healing for the body. We are as strong as the nourishment that we partake into our bodies and our dietary intake allows us to grow and prosper. Food is important to your well-being and determines your success on a daily basis. Many people agree that when they skip meals that they do not think as quickly and cannot perform with the same enthusiasm and motivation. Everyone has a different tolerance level and need to be alert to their boundaries as it relates to food intake. Many have healthcare problems that restrict certain foods or limits the body's ability to process and store. Many have no dietary restrictions but eating too little or too much has negative consequences and changes the flow of our functioning abilities. Healthcare and diet go hand in hand, so when in doubt, always refer to your Healthcare Provider, Primary Care Physician (PCP) or Managed Care Provider. Following a dietary plan that is good for your body image helps to reenergize you at the right time and helps you to slim down in all the right places.

Many food menus are available for persons with diabetes, for vegetarians, vegans or for persons who have ingredient restrictions. When all else fails we can search the internet to get the nourishment that fits our purpose and dietary plans. Many protein drinks and smoothies are available to substitute a meal when we do not have time to prepare as we would prefer. Utilizing these resources allows for quick preparations and relief from hunger and blood sugar elevations or declines. Often, I find myself sluggish during allergy season and discover that a simple fix is to eat a meal and take my prescribed Zyrtec or Certrizine. It's easy to forget what makes us feel better, so having a pill box or calendar alarm will help us maintain focus and live a daily life of vitality. Some have more complicated dietary plans and may need to solicit the support of roommates, family and friends to remain on course with diets and regimens. Healthy eating gives us the stamina we need and ensures we have power to achieve our daily goals.

Libations and Beverages Used Responsibly Keeps Us Hydrated

Libations is the terminology and nice way of discussing alcoholic beverages without making it known to some who may be offended. Drinking water and other beverages are necessary to stay hydrated and to flush out toxins in the body. Drinking too much can cause intoxication, even when drinking too much water. Drinking excessive alcoholic beverages results in intoxication but also has the added severe consequences of impaired decisions, impaired driving and hazardous interactions. You have just achieved a grand milestone, so we certainly don't want to end the celebration with consequences that result in monetary sanctions, restrictions on your ability to drive, serving jail time and hospitalizations. Drinking responsibly will assist you with moving forward and preventing such obstacles to crowd your busy plans to be the best person that you can be. Things happen so quickly, and many persons have died and served life time sentences because they did not drink responsibly, and someone died in a car wreck or by other accidental measures. Heed all the warning signs and plan to be the designated driver or ensure that you set boundaries that allow you to drive to support friends who make the mistake of drinking beyond a legal limit. This is a good time to celebrate, but always remember that it is better to celebrate at home to enjoy the party until completion and plan to celebrate with friends who stay until they are sober and clear to walk or drive. Every decision you make is important to preserving your life and protecting the lives of others.

Chemical Substance Usage, Benefits and the Dangers that Dwell Therein

During this 21st century, usage of marijuana has become more acceptable and legalized within the United States. How we use marijuana also determines the benefits and the dangers that dwell therein. Using marijuana in conjunction with other prescribed medications may have adverse side effects. When using marijuana legally, be certain that you are in an environment that will allow you to remain, in the event that it becomes more toxic than you expected. Many people are in jail for causing accidents under the influence of alcohol. In like manner, many will be incarcerated for using legal marijuana, in the event that reckless driving or accidents occur.

As you celebrate, be alert to date rape drugs and other ways people may lace your drink to get you to engage in behaviors that you may regret or do not prefer in your normal state. Other illegal drugs may be offered to you, but we strongly encourage you to refrain from all illegal drugs and maintain abstinence if you have a predisposition to over indulge. Just say "NO" to drugs and any substance that may alter your mind and mood that is illegal and unhealthy for your well-being. What you do affects everyone around you, and you are accountable for the well-being of others when you are in an altered state that you could have controlled.

So far, the dangers of using chemical substances has more consequences than benefits, so this should give us all a lot to consider. Is it worth the risks? Do I want to spend my life visiting someone in jail because I allowed them to drink and drive and they ended the night in a fatal accident? What if you become severely intoxicated and a friend has a seizure, stroke or has a heart attack and no one is there to take them to the hospital but you? Times like this, we become clear that the choice to drink too much was untimely and sometimes deadly.

Drinking responsibly means making conscious decisions to stop drinking or stop smoking, prior to the point of intoxication. We all have tough decisions to make, so this is your challenge to self-regulate and make the choice to not engage at all or to engage knowing the full consequences and legal ramifications. Always take time to enjoy your friends and family. You will need their support for your lifetime. Cheers to the new Graduate!

CONGRATULATIONS GRADUATE!

YOU HAVE ARRIVED AT THE BEACH

NAVIGATING FROM THE BEACH
TO THE BOARDROOM

Part VI: Using Your
Sailboat to Soar

TAMERA FOLEY, PhD • SHARON WADDLE, PhD

PART VI

Using Your Sailboat to Soar

A sailboat is a small boat that uses wind power to propel it forward. Ask yourself, who is in your sailboat? Sailboat passengers may look different today and in the future. Today your family, friends, teachers, sports affiliations, and clubs may be the only people in your sailboat. In the future, passengers may expand to your colleagues, professors, business associates, book club members and others.

How do the passengers in your sailboat help you to soar? Do they give you positive feedback on your accomplishments? Are they available to speak when you are facing challenges in your life? In order for you to soar, you must examine the passengers in your sailboat. Keep in mind that they should have similar goals for your success. They should be positive and encouraging to you to assist in your success in life. They should be honest but not condemning. They should lift you up and help you focus on opportunities. Focusing on hope and providing inspiration is imperative for your passengers to possess. These relationships are key in your sailboat journey.

Building relationships with the passengers in your sailboat is critical. Knowing how to build and nurture a relationship is work but it is worth it.

Axner, (1993) shares the following steps to building relationships.

1. "Build relationships one at a time.
2. Be friendly and make a connection.
3. Ask people questions.
4. Tell people about yourself.
5. Go places and do things.
6. Accept people the way they are.
7. Assume the people want to form relationships, too.
8. Overcome your fear of rejection.
9. Be persistent.
10. Invite people to get involved.
11. Enjoy people."

Building relationships with people of different cultures, Axner, (1993) adds the following:

1. "Learn about the person's culture.
2. Put yourself at the center of another person's culture.
3. Take a stand about the person's oppression.
4. It's okay to make mistakes."

These steps will assist in building relationships with people now and as you sail and soar in your sailboat.

Having the right people in your sailboat requires relationship building in order to soar. You may own a Honda, a Hummer, a yacht, a boat, a ship, a schooner, a Buick, Cadillac, Kawasaki, an airplane, ski jets or a bicycle.

In like manner, your gifts and special talents will vary with each unique person. Never compare your skills to those of others. You will find new tools in your craftsman toolbox as you allow your creativity to rise to fit the occasion suited to what you have to offer.

Your talent may be as an excellent negotiator, but another person may have great marketing and technology skills. One person may be a great driver and another a renowned speaker. Typically, your work partner has special talents that add value to yours. Be free to allow someone else to shine and soar, because your season is coming.

Take the time to use all of your talents, vehicles and sailboats to soar to success. Congratulations!

CONGRATULATIONS GRADUATE!

YOU HAVE ARRIVED AT THE BEACH

NAVIGATING FROM THE BEACH
TO THE BOARDROOM

Part VII: Your Spiritual Yearnings

TAMERA FOLEY, PhD • SHARON WADDLE, PhD

PART VII

Your Spiritual Yearnings

Our hearts desire and spiritual yearnings are to live a life that brings all of the fruits of the spirit. "But the fruit of the spirit is love, joy, peace, forbearance, kindness, goodness, faithfulness, gentleness and self-control. Against such things there is no law" (Galatians 5: 22-23, New International Version). When you operate in the fruits of the spirit no confrontational problems will occur. Everyone wants to be loved and are happy to receive love even when they have not been loving. Love covers a multitude of sin. We all desire joy and will refrain from making others unhappy when we have joy. When peace surrounds us we are serene and have no legal issues to contend with because peace will always beckon harmony and goodwill. Forbearance is simply the fruit of leniency, patience and self-control. No one goes to the magistrate regarding his ability to defer or forgive, so there is no law against forbearance. Being kind is a treasure that everyone wants to hold onto, so we certainly are not going to give kindness a bad name. Goodness is a spiritual yearning because we need the virtue of looking for the good in life to keep healthy thoughts and a healthy mind. In relationships, partnerships and marriage we want to deal with people who we can depend on and know that they will meet deadlines, pull their load and be available for the long stretch because they are faithful.

Periodically, I receive an iMessage on my iPhone that is sent with "gentle effects", which is done to be certain the tone is noted as a whisper and not as condemnation. Condemnation carries a legal consequence and may cause tempers and emotions to rise negatively, but a whisper tells you the message was sent in love, peace and harmony. Again, there is no law against gentleness. Self-Control, likewise, carries no law because wisdom comes with will-power, whereby we know when to approach and when to retreat. We know when to move forward and when to decline. Self-Control demonstrates that we have no fear, no anxiety and we have assurance that our yearning is to be in peace, containing one's self to be surrounded by calmness and not chaos.

Spiritual Prayer and Meditations

Who we are is defined by our countenance during difficult times. How we respond and react to daily stressors reveals the substance of who we are and who we trust and have confidence in. Too often we trust what the world says about us and lose heart over what people think, say and do. A prayer life will divert the world's way of being right. Meditation and prayer will make straight what seems crooked and awkward in your life and raises you to a new standard. Your meditation and prayer life actually nurture a standard of living on your behalf simply because it changes your thinking to a higher plain. Your prayer life elevates your faith and allows your expectation to rise, whereby you can enjoy the things that you are hoping for. Prayer puts a demand on the power of God to release the treasures for living a spiritual life of harmony, in sync with body, soul and spirit.

Spiritual Worship

We worship when we dance, sing songs of praise and fellowship with persons who have similar spiritual goals and values. Recently, Pastor Cartwright told his congregation that "When you are on the dance floor, throw your hands up and praise God, in the midst". Whether you are dancing to secular song, romance, country music, rhythm and blues or gospel, we are to honor God, who made it all. Praising your creator is how we get repaired and restored. When we want our computers repaired, we honor the manufacturer with a phone call stating our needs and expectations and we put a demand on the company to repair the broken parts and fix any malfunctions. God is our inventor, designer and maker, so who other than He should we call to fix our brokenness? If we fail to call God and worship God, we become useless and hopeless and lose value to be a servant to others. Once again, no matter how long it takes to be redeemed keep going back to the master architect until you are renewed and fit to worship, serve and minister into the lives of others.

Studying for Spiritual Development

In addition to praise and worship, it is important to study scriptures, read meditations daily, watch webinars and listen to audio books, YouTube videos and other methods to bring more knowledge regarding development of your spiritual character. Your brand of self-enrichment may be unique, and your method of teaching and listening can change from day to day. You can listen to biblegateway.com on your iPad, iPod, tablet or other device while on the treadmill or on the track. You can listen in the shower, in the car or simply sitting on the back porch. However you determine to approach spiritual development be sure to pour in and saturate daily because it is your power to stand firm and trust that you can overcome every challenge of the day.

The Graduate Spirit of Leadership

Each of us has a spirit of leadership in the core of our souls that we must develop and aspire to empower. We must develop a passion to fulfill our spiritual purpose and surpass any hindrance or distractions that keep us from the plan and promises of God. We must be grounded to tap into the elite assignments of our spiritual yearnings. We all have a hunger and thirst to be invincible, to surpass the last Guinness Book of Records statistics and to be all that we were created to be. With preparation, faith, courage and power from God we can triumph over every obstacle.

In the book "The Spirit of Leadership", Dr. Myles Munroe notes (2005) that it is essential for true leaders to possess the attitudes and characteristics of: vision, wisdom, decision making, a positive attitude, courage, high energy, personal warmth, humility, righteous anger, integrity, responsibility, a good self-image, friendship, mental horsepower, authority, absence of personal problems, people skills, inspirational power, sense of humor, resilience, track record of experience, passion, self-discipline, creativity, flexibility, sees the big picture, initiative and executive ability. This is a tall order, but each of you are up to the task in your own way. Once you empower yourself to have these gifts you will be able to cope with every challenge in life that comes your way and count it as nothing, to the glory of God.

Spiritual leadership is necessary to bring the world to a greater standard of living and to build nations to the highest level of sovereignty and power. Make melody in your hearts and watch for the fruit of the harvest in every area of your life.

"Therefore, my dear brothers and sisters, stand firm. Let nothing move you. Always give yourselves fully to the work of the Lord, because you know that your labor in the Lord is not in vain" (I Corinthians 15:58, New International Version).

Celebrate the Spirit of Leadership!

CONGRATULATIONS GRADUATE!

YOU HAVE ARRIVED AT THE BEACH

NAVIGATING FROM THE BEACH
TO THE BOARDROOM

Part VIII: Intercepting
Crisis Situations

TAMERA FOLEY, PhD • SHARON WADDLE, PhD

PART VIII

Intercepting Crisis Situations

A highly structured daily routine is often needed to prevent crisis situations. Problems tend to become apparent during idle time when people are more prone to communicate or activate problems that normally would not exist. The most effective strategies for diffusing potentially volatile situations are to simply remove yourself from the environment and make no comments at all regarding the vibes that are occurring. Sometimes you can state why you are leaving when it has nothing to do with the situation that may be brooding, but other times simply walk away. There have been times when I walked into a room and immediately knew that tension was somewhere nearby, so as fast as I entered, I backed out of the room and simply stated, "I've got to leave, there is something I forgot to do". Other times I would go to the bathroom and just leave out the back door saying nothing to anyone.

Good instinct and restfulness will teach you things that you may not be alert to when you are tired, irritable or sluggish for reasons of sickness or fatigue. It is important to choose environments that maintain a steady calm and flow of people who connect with you spiritually. In this age of crime and violence, it takes very little for circumstances to go sour. We are urging you to train for this season and be prepared with an escape plan.

Too often we wear our feelings on our sleeves, and we are offended when we should be concerned about the person who made the comment that disturbed us. Hurt people will often hurt you without knowing it because what they had was hurt and that is all they could think, say or do –hurtful things. We must learn to internalize and be secure in who we are and not be offended by the voice or statements made by others.

Intercepting Offensive Behaviors

Offense may come in the form of text messages, illicit photos, inappropriate gestures, lewd remarks, unkind observations, verbal statements and body language. Offense may manifest into physical confrontation but should never dictate that you reciprocate. Let's toughen up okay. Let's turn the other cheek and laugh it off. After all, we are thick skinned people and we know who we are, so words will not move us and a slap to the face is how they relieve stress (does not have anything to do with you, so choose to walk away and not be offended). The reward for walking away is much greater than the reward for retaliation. Prisons are filled with people who could have just walked away and maintained their freedom.

Offenses may be motivated by behavioral symptoms, psychiatric symptoms, medical reasons or poor and ineffective communication.

Proactive Procedures to Prevent Crisis

To divert crisis situations may include: apologize for all offenses, use comfort statements, comply with basic request to diffuse a problem, be sensitive and alert to the need for environment changes, providing positive reinforcement, reduce demands and back off, use a calm tone of voice, anticipate and redirect conversations and problems, play soothing music, go for walks, exercise and perform fitness activities and plan more frequent breaks.

Behavioral Symptoms

Behavioral issues sometimes cause people to exhibit inappropriate behavior and speak offensive words, name calling or foul terminology because they are seeking attention, bored and want to stir up some excitement or just get caught up with no good reason. Be alert that your behavior, mood and your disposition can be contagious and cause others to react, overreact and end at a place that you did not anticipate. Behavioral symptoms are a choice and should be given thought and care before it moves the conversation from the beach to the courtroom.

Psychiatric Symptoms

Psychiatric Symptoms are typically induced by an internal imbalance, so what starts as a cordial conversation can end up as awkward and disastrous. When something appears to be off or strange, consider that the person may have a mental illness. If the person escalates from 0-10 in a matter of seconds, there is either a miscommunication or a clear issue that needs to be diverted or dismantled. A kind word or any fruits of the spirit can help dismount this situation. Be alert that persons with Bi-Polar Disorder or Schizoaffective Disorder, or other psychiatric diagnoses will have other challenges that contributes to mania and mood swings. Contact the Psychiatrist immediately, if it appears that medications are not managing the behaviors effectively. When all else fails be prepared to seek emergency support or get someone who can help you diffuse the situation and seek emergency medical care.

Medical Symptoms

Medical and physical ailments and illnesses may also serve as the culprit for violent and volatile behaviors that occur in record time or that evolve overtime. Physical ailments, physical disabilities and sensory impairments can cause poor communication, can cause irritability and can cause misunderstandings. Examples of the following medical issues that can evoke crisis situations include but are not limited to vision impairments, hearing impairments, mobility frustrations, and physical ailments.

Vision Impairments

Visual impairments may cause people to see or not see things that are present whereby confusion arises that are difficult to explain. Many times, relationships are impaired because of what someone thought they saw and when they actually saw things that the other person was not aware that they saw or had proof of the situation. It's important to talk to get good understanding and it's important to be truthful and try to rectify problems quickly and calmly. Be careful not to share visual information that can create discord among friends and family. Be a problem solver with diplomacy and love. Be sure to seek ways to get visual check-ups and wear eyewear and contact lenses to support daily vision and academic studies. Being able to see well creates success in all areas of your life and should not be delayed.

Hearing Impairments

Hearing impairments can create another set of problems. People sometime mishear and move forward with the wrong information when they make vital decisions. When in doubt, always repeat what you said and ensure the listener can verbalize back their understanding. Emotions can run high when incorrect information is shared. Be vigilant to have ears tested and get cochlear implants or hearing aids devices to enhance hearing and effective communication. It's important to ask the person to repeat what you said to ensure that you were heard appropriately and that you understood what the hearing-impaired person has communicated to avoid any grief or sorrow.

Mobility Frustrations

Mobility issues can cause a person to be late for appointments and to miss valuable interview and employment, church services and other important events in life. Be certain to assist anyone when time allows and plan more time if you are the person with the mobility problems. It's important to be humble when appointments are missed or delayed. Recently, I was late for an appointment after being delayed in traffic. Because I was more than 15 minutes late, the receptionist informed me that my appointment was cancelled, and I would need to reschedule for another day. Humility and kindness is above the law and the generosity of the healthcare provider allowed me to come back within 2 hours. Some people get upset over little things, but patience can resolve many problems.

Physical Ailments

Physical ailments can run the gamut of emotions and cause screaming and shouting that can be overwhelming and frustrating. Pain can come from many sources and a frown on the face may be misunderstood as mean and angry behavior. Nevertheless, wisdom will always reveal that sickness may be a factor in how a person presents themselves. If you have done nothing to offend a person, never think that the frown is about you or directed at you personally. We all go through pain and distress that mimics angry behavior, so be alert to trust that it is not your fault by any means. When working with persons with disabilities who cannot communicate, we typically watch for signs of discomfort to know whether they have pain or an ailment. All people will eventually point, touch or reveal the areas that hurt by holding the jaw, touching and rubbing the knee or squinting the eyes, etc. Be compassionate and support each other with instructions regarding proper healthcare.

Maturity levels vary among men and women, boys and girls. It's always best to be the bigger person with the most mature attitude. It is in everyone's best interest to remain calm and be productive.

Sensory stimulation issues are also notable and can impact behavioral reactions: 1.) The sense of taste can give us comfort or dissatisfaction when we can no longer taste things. This can be hazardous if we ingest items that are not meant to consume; 2.) The sense of touch is important, but it is important that we not invade personal space, because touching can become offensive; 3.) Our sight allows us to maneuver and get things done. When we cannot see we lose independence and have to learn to depend more on others. Being kind now will ensure that someone is available for the times when we need help. Temperance will invite supports just when we need it. 4.) Hearing is also essential but hearing loss can result in misunderstandings that can result in verbal or physical altercations. Be sure to take measures to ensure good understanding and sufficient communication, 5.) Olfactory sense of smell allows us to recognize when there is smoke, fire or gas odors that warn of impending dangers. The sense of smell also lets us know the smell of good food and good fragrances. Finally, 6.) There are environmental issues all around us that can cause serious problems as it relates to crisis situations. Some places are too hot, too cold, too humid and over time can cause severe distress, impatience and evoke volatile discord. Be prepared to take action to change the environment and find a solution. Maybe a cool down with a wet cloth around your neck, pat your face with a damp cloth, breathe deeply and slowly and dress accordingly.

Anti-Violence Tips

Guns, knives, arson, among other weapons are used for daily domestic crimes and for mass destructions. Many schools and organizations have been threatened with weapons, bombs and mass destructions have hit the community repeatedly nationwide and abroad. Many young people are incarcerated because they do not have the maturity, skills and self-control to use weapons responsibly. If you live in the home with weapons, you are at risk, particularly when children are present and when the owner does not store away and use responsibly. The Division of Law Enforcement Bureau of Forensic Services in the State of California report (2017-2018) that handguns are use in 86% of crimes, rifles in 9% of crimes, and shotguns in 4.5% of crimes. Try to resolve with fruits of the spirit and not using weapons.

School disasters in the USA Mitchell et al (2017) note that, "At the root of each incident is a history of abuse, neglect, bullying, harassment, teasing and victimization." Many other schools, churches and public organizations have also occurred more attacks than we can imagine.

Call for Prayer

For purposes of violence prevention, we contend that the nations must be in prayer for our schools, homes, workplaces, community and for our children.

George Sawyer (2015) Founding Pastor of Calvary Assembly of God in Tanner, AL notes in his book, The Daniel Prayer for Parents, "Prayer can define the destiny of a generation. Never has a generation been as assaulted and abused, both inside and out of the womb, as today's youth. We must recognize and respond to this satanic assault with an even greater intensity and devotion and we must pray for his chosen generation". Praying and calling on the name of Jesus is always good advice and yields the best results. Pastor Sawyer (2015) provides a guide for parents to declare the Daniel prayer blessings over their children:

> *"Father, I come to you right now in Jesus's name, I pray that when my child takes a test or exam, or when he/she is considered for special opportunities, that like Daniel and his friends he will be found ten times better than all, and that none will be found equal.*
>
> *I pray that my child will retain and recall everything he has studied. Because of your favor, my child will be promoted and recognized and have great influence for Christ. I declare that my child is blessed with your supernatural power to fulfill his/her destiny. My child _____, is blessed and no curse can come to rest upon him/her. Again, I pray this in Jesus's name. Amen."*

We declare a blessing of favor, honor and dominion over the nations and pray for international peace in Jesus name.

ALERTS* To Prevent Crisis

People should avoid finger pointing, hand pointing and avoid making demands. DO NOT SCOLD others nor talk in a harsh tone of voice. Be courteous, non-threatening and non-confrontational. Also be alert that behavioral symptoms and psychiatric symptoms have different criteria and concerns. We urge you to avoid putting your hands on your hip and shaking your fingers because it can result in adverse consequences. Often, it's best to just walk away.

Please be professional, courteous, dependable and have excellent work ethics for continual success in life.

Prevention and Response to Legal Issues

Please be informed regarding laws of your local community and state to avoid receiving a fine, violation ticket or being arrested. If you are apprehended or arrested for any reason, do not resist arrest. DO NOT

SPEAK until your family sends an attorney or public defender. Many young men and women fall in the trap of saying things that are used against them in courts. Today American prisons are over-crowded with innocent young people who spoke and were given years to serve and/or life in prison. Never admit to any crime, because there may be circumstances that you are not aware of when the crime occurs. Be sure the attorney you choose does not have a history with or bias to the adversary. This may be very prevalent in small communities.

Be alert that the justice system can make mistakes and have human flaws whereby ethics, integrity and humanity are not always drivers for important judicial decisions. Be alert that many innocent people are incarcerated for a lifetime because they were in the wrong place. Remember that the mental illness and true criminals can be rehabilitated. Avoid the appearance of evil, means guarding yourself, containing yourself and dismissing your presence from volatile environments and atmospheres. Compel your state legislators to upgrade laws and ethical rulings to ensure empathy and compassion for humans who are mentally ill and for all people to live in Humane environments, when incarcerated. To move forward we need to become less punitive and more restorative to build a better society.

Restitution: If you destroy, damage or break the property of another person, be quick to pay for items or have the items repaired. Restore any environment that you have disturbed and be sincere and apologetic.

Suicide Protocol: If you suspect that any person that you know has suicidal tendencies, be sure to have them monitored closely. If a person makes threats of harm to self, immediate action should be taken to get professional help. A special no harm contract and/or assessment for hospitalization should be done as quickly as possible.

Elopement and Missing Persons: When persons are missing from their home or assigned areas, be aware of procedures to follow and report immediately. Note all clothing items that the person is wearing in order to assist with finding he/she in the event of their absence/elopement. Local police departments should be contacted regarding persons who are lost or missing. Most importantly call family and friends to make them aware of the status of a missing person.

Human Trafficking: Human trafficking is prevalent in every state in the United States. California, Texas and Florida are the top 3 most critically hit areas; however, trafficking occurs in every town and city all over the world. Human trafficking is a modern-day form of slavery whereby people are illegally trading for services and sex acts. Sex trafficking has become a crisis in America, and it is important to watch children, teenagers and young adults closely and do not let them out of reach of a responsible friend, parent, teacher or authority. Immediately report any suspicious activity. Trafficking task forces have been developed in most all states and regions of the state to increase awareness and support for persons who are able to escape. Human life is valuable and should be guarded and protected by every measure necessary. We have a responsibility to report suspicious activities as it relates to trafficking of drugs, people and all lewd and unethical and illegal behaviors.

Infant Deaths: Recent infant deaths have risen in America and has become critical to communicate to all parents the importance of not leaving children in the car alone at any time nor any season of the year. To prevent forgetting the child is present in the car be sure to place items on the seat that will be needed to lock doors or enter in buildings that you will arrive at. Be certain to put your lunch or handbag in the back seat with the child, so that you will have reminders (set alarms on your watch daily) to ensure child safety is always of utmost importance.

Preserving Human Rights and Dignity

Everyone wants to be treated with respect and dignity. It's important to be humane and act with kindness to all people at all times. Ethical behavior and integrity make more opportunities to live on the level of the boardroom while hanging out at the beach just to have fun. Keep life simple and you will have the reward of a good life.

CONGRATULATIONS GRADUATE!

YOU HAVE ARRIVED AT THE BEACH

NAVIGATING FROM THE BEACH
TO THE BOARDROOM

Part IX: Personal Goals and Expectations for Life

TAMERA FOLEY, PhD • SHARON WADDLE, PhD

PART IX

Personal Goals and Expectations for Life

Setting Goals

Setting Goals is a process that can assist you in getting to the beach. Goals help you to keep your vision and make a commitment for success. We should have goals in life. Let's think about whether we want to engage in a service occupation to help others. We may want to engage in a highly demanding occupation or become an entrepreneur and own your own business. To achieve any of these choices you must have goals.

Goals should possess the following characteristics:

1. Specific
2. Measurable
3. Attainable
4. Relevant
5. Time specific

These characteristics address what is referred to as SMART Goals.

State each goal with a positive statement. Be precise about what you want to achieve. Prioritize your goals. Keep goals small so you can reach them and then set another set of goals. Ensure that your goals are realistic and achievable.

First, you must determine your goals. Take time to think, pray, and write them down. Then visualize your goals. Ask yourself, do these goals align with your morals and values? Secondly, are your goals reasonable? Remember that goals should be reasonable and achievable. Thirdly, share your goals with someone you can trust. Discuss them with a person(s) and ask them to hold you accountable.

Being held accountable to your goals can help you achieve and meet your expectations for life. Many people develop a vision board. This board can be photos of words to assist you in keeping your priorities so that you can achieve your goals. It is a visual picture of your wants, needs, and desires. It helps you to think and visualize your life expectations.

Financial Responsibility

Having goals in life also mean that you must not forget to be financially responsible. What is your financial goal? Financial responsibility is how you manage your money. Preparing a budget is useful to see how much money you have to manage. It is important to know what you are spending money on and tracking your spending is critical. Making the right decisions early in life will assist in your future. Learning about investments, savings, having an emergency fund, managing debt, using credit wisely are all areas of financial responsibility. There are experts that can and will assist you in these areas.

Early career debt may lower your credit score and make it difficult to purchase a home, car or other essential items at an affordable interest rate. Too much debt may be a hindrance to securing job opportunities, because many employers now conduct credit checks to surmise fiscal responsibility prior to hiring. Debt late in your career could mean working longer because you cannot retire, it may mean not being able to start a business because you don't have enough capital or good credit, or it may induce stress. Depending on your circumstances, debt may delay you from completing your career goals.

Expectations for Life

When you have followed good counseling on budgeting and spending habits, you can rest well, knowing you are prepared for the sweet things that bring joy in life. Remember that life may not always go as you planned. There will be bumps in the road. Planning and having expectations will assist you in achieving your goals so you can enjoy the beach kind of life.

CONGRATULATIONS GRADUATE!

YOU HAVE ARRIVED AT THE BEACH

NAVIGATING FROM THE BEACH
TO THE BOARDROOM

Part X: Continuous
Self-Improvement

TAMERA FOLEY, PhD • SHARON WADDLE, PhD

PART X

Continuous Self-Improvement

As you travel on your journey to the beach continuous self-improvement will be a part of the learning process. We may learn through books, experiences, conversations with others, the media, and many other ways. We want to improve our learning, grow, and become better each day, month, and year of our lives.

Continuous Self-Improvement

Continuous self-improvement must be intentional. You may want to focus on one small thing. Learn about that one thing and put an action plan in place for self-improvement. Write down the steps it will take to ensure you meet your target. Some areas will take practice and perseverance. Remember to take baby steps so you can remain focused.

Continuous self-improvement means taking the time to celebrate when you have met your target. Then set a new target to achieve. In doing this you will face your fears or areas that you are not comfortable. Work on conquering your fears. What will it take and who do you need as support? You will make mistakes along the way and that is okay as long as you can admit them and learn from them. Keeping a focus and believing you can improve is a big hurdle that you can achieve. You are investing in yourself and in being better.

Enrichment of Study Habits

Enrichment of study habits begin with embracing a positive attitude. Choose a place to study that meets your studying style. Ensure that you have all the necessary materials that you need to reduce any down time. If you have to read or review any notes, it may be beneficial to make an outline. Some people find it necessary to write the important points to help them remember. Using mnemonic devices helps you with word association. Having someone quiz you or using note cards to quiz yourself is another way to help you remember. People also use study groups which can be helpful. It is essential to find out your style and utilize it on your journey to the beach of self-improvement.

Continuous self-improvement and enrichment of study habits are part of beach life that will always be a positive part of your life. Embrace it and take the time to grow. We are all born with potential. Greatness is in your DNA, heritage, and genetic make-up. Choose to exercise your greatness. You are the next great influencer in the world. You are resilient, so prepare to use your ambitions to succeed.

CONGRATULATIONS GRADUATE!

YOU HAVE ARRIVED AT THE BEACH

NAVIGATING FROM THE BEACH
TO THE BOARDROOM

Part XI: Turning on the Lighthouse to Your Dreams and Ambitions

TAMERA FOLEY, PhD • SHARON WADDLE, PhD

PART XI

Turning on the Lighthouse to Your Dreams and Ambitions

According to the National Park Services, a lighthouse has two purposes. One purpose is that it serves as a navigational aid. The second purpose is that it warns boats of dangerous areas. Prior to technology used today, the lighthouses had bells, cannons, horns that they utilized to warn the ships. And that also served as a resource to seamen. Some seaman still utilizes lighthouses as they are important when their technology is down.

Manifesting your dreams requires brainstorming for ideas, work, research, study, drive and motivation. Building your lighthouse may require a ladder or someone to hold you up during turbulent times. Perseverance and being steadfast among other preparations will ignite the switch that turns on your lighthouse to good living.

According to Psychology Today (2019), "Dreams are the stories the brain tells during sleep - collections of clips, images, feelings, and memories that involuntarily occur during the rapid eye movement (REM) stage of slumber. People often dream when they have a strong desire to achieve something (ambition)".

As we dream about all the possibilities that life affords us, we must be aware of the horns and bells that warn us along the way. We have a lighthouse in our brain that helps us to navigate our sailboat on the right course. It assists us in making the right turn, so we don't run into danger. We will need to make decisions as we work towards our ambitions. Some warning will be visible to the naked eye while others will require investigation.

Langston Hughes (1994) wrote the poem "Dreams". He was a great poet, novelist, fiction writer and playwright.

> Dreams
> Hold fast to dreams
> For if dreams die
> Life is a broken winged bird
> That cannot fly.
>
> Hold fast to dreams
> For when dreams go
> Life is a barren field
> Frozen with snow.

Ensure that your dreams and ambitions are aligned with your goals, that they are a part of healthy living, they are a part of your continual self-improvement plan. Heed to the lighthouse along the way as you work towards your ambitions in life. Continue to dream!

SUMMARY: NAVIGATING FROM THE BEACH TO THE BOARDROOM

We desire that you read this book, subtitle "Navigating from the Beach to the Boardroom" and share additional copies with all the graduates you know to prepare them for the next journey and seasons of life.

The beach and boardroom represent unison in mind, body, soul and spirit. It represents being your brother's keeper. It is ingrained in the heart of academic success and mental health that is contagious all over the nations.

As school counselors, practitioners, spiritual leaders, educators and disciplinarians we want to shout out to the world that we can overcome the pain and suffering that we are going through. We can reduce crime rates and financial stressors, illicit sexual abductions and every problem that holds us back from freedom and liberty. We will be more alert; we will strive all day every day to be more astute and prepared to react and proactively plan ways to master the environmental schemas around us. We will be strategic and prepared for life and good living.

It is our desire that the students will share this information with their families, friends, and persons they want to mentor to better equip them for safe and secure living with compelling success. We wanted to ensure that students everywhere are provided with resources that they have never been exposed to in one venue to perpetuate mountain moving success in every area of life.

Look up, laugh and love because the beach is bringing a tidal wave of joy, peace and success your way.

Until Next Time. See you at the Beach!

REFERENCES

Axner, M. (1993). *The community leadership project curriculum.* Pomfret: CT. The Topsfield Foundation.

Becerra, X. (2017-2018) *Biennial Report.* Division of Law Enforcement Bureau of Forensic Services. Retrieved from http://oag.ca.gov/publications#crime

Brues, M., Brenner, G., Wenk, G., & Bulkeley, K. (2019). *Why we dream.* Psychology Today, Sussex Publishers, LLC.

Fall is back to-school time: top 5 things to consider when choosing a career. (2015, August). Retrieved from https://www.artistic.edu/top-5-things-to-consider-when-choosing-a-career/

Garnett, Laura (2019). *The genius habit: how one habit can radically change your work and your life. 15 of the greatest graduation speeches of all times.* Sourcebook, Inc.

Retrieved from https://www.inc.com/laura-garnett/15-of-the-greatest-graduation-speeches-of-all-time.html

Gray, M. (2015). *Five reasons why having a social life is significant while balancing your academics.* Retrieved from https://www.theodysseyonline.com/five-reasons-why-having-social-life-significant

How to choose a career. (2018). Retrieved from www.careerkey.org/choose-a-career/how-to-cjppse-a-career.html

Hughes, L. (1994). *The collected poems of Langston Hughes.* Published by Alfred A. Knopf/Vintage. Retrieved from https://poets.org › poet › Langston-Hughes

Mitchell, M., Longhurst, J., Jacob, D., Allen, D. and Soma, C. (2017). *Violence in Schools: What Matters Most.* Retrieved from www.star.org

Munroe, M. (2005). *The spirit of leadership: cultivating the attitudes that influence human action.* New Kingston, PA: Whitaker House.

Potter, D. (2019) *Texting etiquette: a brief guide to polite messaging.* Retrieved from https://www.grammarly.com › blog › texting-etiquette

Sawyer, G. (2015). *The Daniel prayer for parents: praying favor, protection, and blessing over your children.* Lake Mary, Florida: Charisma House.

ABOUT THE AUTHOR

MEET DR. TAMERA FOLEY

Dr. Foley began her professional career in education in Unit District Number Five in Normal, Illinois as a Special Education Resource Teacher in 1981. She then moved back to her hometown of Rockford, Illinois and spent fifteen years in the Rockford Public School District in various roles: Cross Categorical Special Education Teacher, Fifth Grade Teacher, and Assistant Director of Saturday School, Director of Saturday School, Assistant Principal, Principal, and Special Education Coordinator. During the fifteen years, she continuously participated in and conducted trainings. She also completed her Masters' Degree and her Administration Degree. Dr. Foley was awarded with the Golden Apple for Excellence in Teaching, Distinguished Educator Award from the Rockford Branch of the NAACP, Special Thanks for Special People Award from the Parent Council of Rockford Schools, and the For Kids' Sake Award.

In 2005, she was afforded the opportunity to join Clayton County Public Schools as the Secondary Director of Special Education. As a life-long learner, she has presented to students in Limon, Costa Rica through an invitation from the United States Embassy. Dr. Foley spent a month exploring special education supports and services in Hungary and the Czech Republic through a Fulbright Scholarship. She has held various positions in Clayton County to include Director of Learning Support, Director of Student Services, and served as the Executive Director of Teaching and Learning. Dr. Foley has lead district initiatives such as the implementation of the school-based health center-The Family Health Center at North Clayton High School, Asthma Friendly School Initiative, Positive Behavior Interventions and Supports, Implementation of Kurzweil to improve student and parent literacy, dropout prevention, literacy, and others initiatives that have a direct impact on the teaching and learning of students in Clayton County Public Schools. Dr. Foley has also worked as Regional Director for the Alabama Department of Mental Health Division of Developmental Disabilities since leaving the school system.

Dr. Foley is a life-long learner. She currently is an Independent Consultant who is passionate about her work and is an advocate of all students.

ABOUT THE AUTHOR

MEET DR. SHARON WADDLE

Dr. Waddle reside in Athens Alabama and she enjoys country living, beautiful trees and flowers blooming in all colors. She likes sitting on her back porch with friends talking and watching her neighbors' roses in full bloom while talking about the sweet things in life. She likes to sing, plan parties and create unique ideas. She likes writing because it is relaxing and takes her to a sovereign place of peace. Her best ideas come when she is resting and spending moments meditating and trusting God. Dr. Waddle enjoys helping friends become successful, when they have projects bigger than themselves. Gospel music and jazz gives her joy and lifts her spirit. She is a woman of faith and she believes in and demand freedom and liberty for all humanity.

Dr. Sharon Waddle completed a terminal degree in Industrial Organizational Psychology from Capella University. She is proud to be a two-time alumnus of Alabama A & M University where she earned a masters' degree in Clinical Psychology. She worked diligently as a Psychologist for the Alabama Department of Mental Health for 30 years. She is a member of the Society for Industrial Organizational Psychologist, the National Association for People of Color and is a member of Delta Sigma Theta Sorority Incorporated.

She is founder and owner of Simply Sovereign Consulting Firm, started in 2014 with a focus on inspirational book writing, behavioral and psychological consulting and assisting community organizations with ministry programs and conference planning. Dr. Waddle is the author of "How Companies Manage during the Healthcare Crisis (2012); Simply Sovereign: Birthing out the Promise (2014) and Whisper: Word to the Wise (2016). Her forthcoming book is a devotional entitled "Pray Mightily: Your Prayers Have Kept Me Alive.

Dr. Sharon Malone Waddle

Printed in the United States
By Bookmasters